# Catching
## the
# Moon

### The Story of a Young Girl's Baseball Dream

by Crystal Hubbard

illustrated by Randy DuBurke

Lee & Low Books Inc.
New York

LEE & LOW BOOKS Inc., 95 Madison Avenue, New York, NY 10016
leeandlow.com

Manufactured in China by Jade Productions

Book design by Christy Hale
Book production by The Kids at Our House

The text is set in Transitional 551 Medium
The illustrations are rendered in pen and ink and acrylic

(HC) 10 9 8 7 6 5 4
(PB) 15 14 13 12 11 10 9
First Edition

Library of Congress Cataloging-in-Publication Data
Hubbard, Crystal.
Catching the moon: the story of a young girl's baseball dream /
by Crystal Hubbard ; illustrated by Randy DuBurke.— 1st ed.
p. cm.
Summary: "A picture book biography highlighting a pivotal event in the
childhood of African American baseball player Marcenia 'Toni Stone' Lyle
Alberga, the woman who broke baseball's gender barrier by becoming the
first female roster member of a professional Negro League team"
—Provided by publisher.
ISBN 978-1-58430-243-8 (HC)   ISBN 978-1-60060-572-7 (PB)
1. Stone, Toni, 1921–1996. 2. Baseball players—United States—
Biography—Juvenile literature. 3. African American baseball play-
ers—Biography—Juvenile literature. 4. Women baseball players—United
States—Biography—Juvenile literature. I. DuBurke, Randy, ill. II. Title.
GV865.S86H83 2005
796.357'092—dc22                          2004028559

### ACKNOWLEDGMENTS
Special acknowledgment must be made to the Negro Leagues Baseball Museum
in Kansas City, Missouri; the National Baseball Hall of Fame and Museum in
Cooperstown, New York; the Oakland Museum of California; David Cataneo;
Sully; Buck O'Neill; Albert Gough; Connie Morgan; and Marcenia "Toni Stone"
Lyle Alberga.

### AUTHOR'S SOURCES
#### BOOKS
Berlage, Gai Ingham. Women in Baseball: The Forgotten History. Westport,
    Connecticut: Greenwood Publishing Group, Inc., 1994.
Bruce, Janet. The Kansas City Monarchs: Champions of Black Baseball.
    Lawrence, Kansas: University Press of Kansas, 1985.
Peterson, Robert. Only the Ball Was White: A History of Legendary Black Players
    and All-Black Professional Teams. New York: McGraw-Hill, 1984.
Rogosin, Donn. Invisible Men: Life in Baseball's Negro Leagues. New York:
    Atheneum, 1983.

#### MAGAZINE ARTICLES
"Woman Player Says 'Could Take Care of Self' in Games." Ebony, June-July
    1953, 50.

#### NEWSPAPER ARTICLES
Blass, Tony. "Baseball Pioneer Tells Students to Follow Dreams." St. Paul
    Pioneer Press Dispatch, March 7, 1990.
DuBay, Diane. "From St. Paul Playgrounds to Big Leagues, Stone Always Loved
    Baseball." Minnesota Women's Press, February 1993, 3–16.

#### INTERVIEWS
Gough, Albert. Telephone Interview. January 11, 1996.
O'Neill, Buck. Personal Interview. January 18, 1996.

#### ADDITIONAL READING
McKissack, Patricia C. and Fredrick, Jr. Black Diamond: The Story of the Negro
    Baseball Leagues. New York: Scholastic, 1994.
Winter, Jonah. Fair Ball! 14 Great Stars From Baseball's Negro Leagues. New
    York: Scholastic Press, 1999.

To Melvin Miller, who saw in me what I didn't know I had—C.H.

To my lovely and very patient wife, Olivia,
and our two wonderful boys,
Sakai and Matthias, with love—R.D.

Marcenia Lyle loved baseball.

She loved the powdery taste of dust clouds as she slid through them. She loved the way the sun heated her hair as she crouched in the outfield, waiting for fly balls. And she loved the sting in her palm as a baseball slammed into it, right before tagging a runner out.

If there was anything in the world better than baseball, Marcenia didn't know what it was. She dreamed of growing up to be a professional ballplayer, so she could play all the time.

"I wish I knew why you liked baseball so much." Mama sighed as she gently washed Marcenia's hair.

Marcenia shrugged. Mama often questioned Marcenia's interest in baseball, particularly when washing field dirt from her hair.

"It's just fun," Marcenia said, giving her mother the same response she always did.

"Playing dolls is fun," Mama said.

Marcenia blew a puff of lather from her palm. "Not as much fun as baseball."

After Marcenia crawled into bed, Papa appeared in the doorway.

"What did you learn in school today?" he asked.

"Ummm . . ." Marcenia thought for a moment. "Some history?"

Papa crossed his arms. "And how did your team do in the game after school?"

"Harold got a triple in his first at bat, and Clarence tagged out two runners," Marcenia said eagerly. "I struck out my first time at bat, but then I caught a deep fly ball that would have scored the tying run for the other team if I'd missed it. We won, 11–10."

Marcenia's smile gleamed like the noonday sun as she shared the details of her victory.

"We won the game," Marcenia said once more.

"And you also ripped another dress," Papa said, dismayed. Then he kissed Marcenia's cheek and turned off the light, leaving her alone with moonlight and shadows and her dream of becoming a baseball player.

The tiny house was still. Marcenia could almost hear her mother's needle and thread moving through the fabric as she sat at the kitchen table mending Marcenia's dress.

After a while Marcenia heard Papa's voice. "I wish she would think about school as much as she thinks on baseball."

"She wants to be a ballplayer when she grows up," Mama said with a sad chuckle. "I just want her to be happy."

"She'll be what every other girl in this neighborhood will be," Papa grumbled. "A teacher, a nurse, or— "

"A maid," Mama said softly.

"I'm going to score three runs tomorrow," Marcenia promised the darkness as she clapped her hands over her ears. "I'm going to hit a home run too."

The next day after school, Marcenia went to the playground. The other girls stayed on the hardtop to play hopscotch, jump rope, or jacks. The boys were huddled at the mound, talking quietly. They cast excited glances at a man who was watching the field from the bleachers.

"Do you know who he is?" Harold asked Marcenia as she joined the group. He tipped his head toward the man. "That there is Mr. Gabby Street. He's running a baseball day camp this summer."

Marcenia knew about Gabby Street. He was the manager for the St. Louis Cardinals. He had led his Cardinals to the National League pennant in 1930, and the Cardinals had topped that the next year by winning the 1931 World Series.

"What's he want?" Marcenia asked.

"Kids for his baseball camp," Harold said. "It's going to be right here on this field every day except Sunday. Sundays are game days."

"What's it cost?" Marcenia asked.

"It's free-e-e!" said Clarence.

"All you need is your own glove and baseball cleats," Harold added.

Marcenia could hardly contain her excitement. She would do anything to be one of the players in Mr. Street's camp!

That afternoon Marcenia played with a purpose. She scooped grounders, catching them into her body to make sure they didn't bounce away.

She slid into second, keeping low so she wouldn't be tagged. She kept her eyes on each pitch, waiting for a good one to send over the fence.

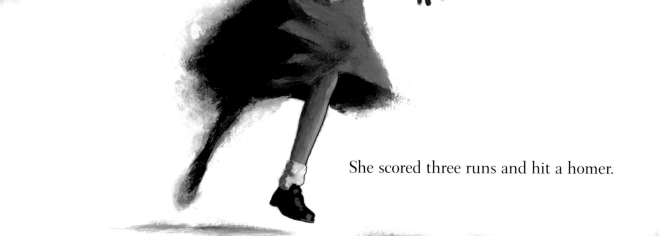

She scored three runs and hit a homer.

When Mr. Street approached the players after the game, Marcenia crowded in close so he could see her.

"I just saw some good ball," Mr. Street said, smiling. "Who wants to come to my baseball camp and really learn to play this game?"

Every hand went up.

Mr. Street shook them all. He shook Marcenia's hand last. "You've got a good arm, little miss, and you run fast," he said. "But I don't take girls in my camp."

Marcenia looked down so no one would see her disappointment.
She began striking dust from her dress.

"Marcenia's been playing ball with us since we were little kids,"
Harold told Mr. Street.

"She's the only player we got who ever steals bases," Clarence said.

Marcenia was pleased that her friends had come to her defense, but
Mr. Street didn't change his mind. As she walked home, she thought
about how these very same boys had teased her when she first started
playing baseball with them. Then when they saw she could run, hit, and
throw as well as they could, the teasing stopped. They had let her play.

Marcenia decided to give Mr. Street a reason to change his mind.

Everyday Marcenia played baseball, and everyday Mr. Street refused to invite her to his camp. Then came a day when Marcenia got tired of hearing him say, "I don't take girls in my camp." That day, when she was on third base in the ninth inning of a tie game, Marcenia decided to take the biggest chance in all baseball. She decided to steal home.

When the pitcher drew back his arm to throw the ball to Harold, Marcenia launched into motion.

The catcher snared the pitch in his glove and ran toward Marcenia to tag her out. Marcenia doubled back toward third. When the catcher threw the ball back to the third baseman, Marcenia turned and bolted toward home plate. As the ball sailed above her head, Marcenia pumped her arms and knees harder.

With the ball speeding toward home, Marcenia dropped her weight and slid into home plate. She had stolen home and scored the winning run!

While her teammates celebrated their victory, Marcenia planted her hands on her hips and faced Mr. Street.

"I am a baseball player," she said. "I want to learn to play this game as well as I can. May I come to your camp?"

"Well, little miss, if you can steal home, you can probably do anything you set your mind to," Mr. Street said. "You can come to my camp as long as you have your equipment."

When Marcenia told her parents the good news about the camp that evening, her father was not pleased.

"I don't like you acting like such a tomboy," he said with a snap of his evening paper. "Besides, you know we don't have money to spend on—"

"The camp's free!" Marcenia said excitedly.

"Equipment isn't free," Papa said.

"I have a glove," Marcenia said. "Harold gave me his old one."

"You'll need cleats, and we don't have money for those," Papa added. "So unless you're prepared to get them yourself, I think you'll have to forget about that camp."

With another snap of Papa's newspaper, Marcenia felt her dream move out of reach.

Mr. Street was at the field the next time Marcenia played. Before the game, she mustered all her strength to keep from crying.

"Mr. Street," she said, "I can't come to your camp. I don't have cleats and my father says we can't afford them. But thank you for inviting me."

Although she was sad, Marcenia played as well as she always had. She loved baseball too much not to play with all her heart.

That night, unable to sleep, Marcenia gazed through her window at the full moon glowing in the sky. It was so round and bright, like a brand new baseball. She reached to the floor and took up her baseball glove. She put it on and punched the pocket, as if the moon would drop into it like so many fly balls had before.

Marcenia wondered sadly if Papa was right. Maybe girls didn't grow up to be ballplayers after all. But playing baseball was her dream, and Marcenia couldn't imagine doing anything else.

The next day after school Marcenia was the first one at the playing field. Mr. Street was already there, and he waved Marcenia over.

"You're a good ballplayer, Marcenia," he said. "I want good ballplayers for my camp."

He handed Marcenia a box, and he watched as she opened it. Her eyes widened as she pulled out a shoe with each hand. These weren't just any shoes. These were real baseball cleats!

"Thank you, Mr. Street!" Marcenia was so excited she could barely squeeze out the words. She hugged the shoes to her chest. They were even better than stealing home!

"Don't you have a game to play?" Mr. Street said, nodding toward the field.

"Yes, I do!" Marcenia replied happily. Her fingers flew as they unbuckled her street shoes and laced on her new cleats. They fit perfectly. She ran in them. She jumped in them. She caught and slid in them. And she hit a home run in them.

After the game the boys rushed to Mr. Street, talking over one another about the game. Marcenia lingered at home plate. She stared at her feet, proud of the new scuffs and smudges on her shoes. They had been a little stiff at first. But now that she had played a good game of baseball in them, the cleats were exactly the way she wanted them to be.

Mr. Street excused himself from the crowd of boys. "I look forward to seeing you in camp," he said to Marcenia.

She gave him a hopeful smile, but Marcenia knew she still had one more person to convince before she could officially accept Mr. Street's invitation. She ran home and waited anxiously for her father to return from work.

As soon as her father arrived, Marcenia showed him her new cleats.

"Now, Marcenia, where did you get those shoes?" Papa asked sternly.

"Mr. Street gave them to me," Marcenia said. "He wants me to come to his baseball camp."

Papa looked down at Marcenia's baseball cleats, which were already scuffed and dusted with field dirt.

"You must be a pretty good ballplayer for an important man like Mr. Street to buy you those shoes," he admitted. Then he smiled.

"You know I don't like charity, but I reckon we can't give those shoes back in this state. I'll have to thank Mr. Street for his generosity when I take you down to that baseball camp."

Marcenia could hardly believe her ears—Papa had agreed! Her chest
filled with joy and she threw her arms around her father, hugging him hard.

"You'll see how good I am!" she cried.

Marcenia felt as proud and happy as if she had reached right up in the
sky and caught the moon in her glove. She was on her way to becoming a
real baseball player. She would make her dream come true.

# Afterword

MARCENIA LYLE never lost her passion for baseball or her dream of playing professionally. In 1937, at the age of sixteen, she began her career as a pitcher with the Twin Cities Colored Giants. From there she moved on to semiprofessional and minor league Negro teams, including the San Francisco Sea Lions and the New Orleans Creoles. As Marcenia's playing career took off, she changed her name to Toni Stone. The name Marcenia "was just too cute for baseball," she said.

In 1953, when she was thirty-two years old, Toni's dream of playing professional baseball came true. She signed to play second base for the Negro League Indianapolis Clowns, filling the position vacated by Hank Aaron's move to the Major Leagues. This made Toni the first female member of an all-male professional baseball team. One of the highlights of her career came that same year in an Easter Sunday game in Omaha, Nebraska. Toni Stone was the only player that day to get a hit off Satchel Paige, one of the best pitchers in the history of the sport.

Photograph courtesy of the Negro Leagues Baseball Museum, Inc.

No matter how hard she worked to prove she belonged, Toni always felt like the outsider—the woman playing a "man's game." "I just loved the game," she once said. "But they weren't ready for me. So many of them thought it was a disgrace to play with a girl. But my heart was set. And I kept at it. You gotta keep trying."

Toni finished her professional career with the Kansas City Monarchs, retiring after the 1954 season. She settled into married life with her husband, Colonel Aurelious Pescia Alberga, and continued to play recreational baseball until she was sixty-two years old.

Marcenia "Toni Stone" Lyle Alberga died on November 2, 1996, at the age of seventy-five. She had no children of her own, but today girls and boys play on a field named after her at the Dunning playground in St. Paul, Minnesota. Toni Stone was inducted into the Women's Sports Hall of Fame and is honored in the Women in Baseball exhibit and the Negro Leagues section in the National Baseball Hall of Fame in Cooperstown, New York.